电子科技系列科普绘本
Serial Pop Science Picture Books on Electronic Sci-tech

你知道与不知道的 HOW MUCH DO YOU KNOW ABOUT

电子测量仪器

ELECTRONIC MEASURING INSTRUMENTS?

（中英对照版）

(Chinese-English Version)

赵 轲 主编　　Written by: Ke Zhao

赵 轲 龙 梅 郝聪婷 翻译　　Translated by: Ke Zhao　Mei Long　Congting Hao

电子科技大学出版社
University of Electronic Science and Technology of China Press
· 成都 ·

图书在版编目（CIP）数据

你知道与不知道的电子测量仪器：汉英对照 / 赵轲

主编. -- 成都：成都电子科大出版社，2024. 12.

ISBN 978-7-5770-1484-5

Ⅰ. TM93-49

中国国家版本馆 CIP 数据核字第 2025EK3920 号

你知道与不知道的电子测量仪器（中英对照版）

NI ZHIDAO YU BUZHIDAO DE DIANZI CELIANG YIQI (ZHONG-YING DUIZHAO BAN)

赵轲　主编

策划编辑　谢忠明　黄杨杨

责任编辑　蒋　伊

责任校对　段晓静

责任印制　段晓静

出版发行　电子科技大学出版社
　　　　　成都市一环路东一段 159 号电子信息产业大厦九楼　邮编 610051

主　　页　www.uestcp.com.cn

服务电话　028-83203399

邮购电话　028-83201495

印　　刷　成都久之印刷有限公司

成品尺寸　250 mm×250 mm

印　　张　2

字　　数　46 千字

版　　次　2024 年 12 月第 1 版

印　　次　2024 年 12 月第 1 次印刷

书　　号　ISBN 978-7-5770-1484-5

定　　价　36.00 元

创作团队　CREATION TEAM

顾问　CONSULTANT

陈德利

Deli Chen

儿童顾问　CHILDREN CONSULTANT

陈昕悦

Xinyue Chen

作者　WRITER

赵　轲

Ke Zhao

创作人员　OTHER CREATORS

郝聪婷	王念慈	叶桂兰
Congting Hao	Nianci Wang	Guilan Ye

设计制作　DESIGNER

付学瑞	汤伟东
Xuerui Fu	Weidong Tang

AR 开发　AR DEVELOPER

苏州和云观博数字科技有限公司

Suzhou AR-Museum Digital Technology Co. , Ltd.

AR 读本这样用
How to Use the AR Books?

1 用手机或平板扫描上方二维码，下载"云观博"APP。

Scan the QR code with your smart phones or pads, and download the "AR-Museum" app.

2 选择"社教"中的"电子科技博物馆 AR 读本"，点击"AR"功能。

Select "the Electronic Science and Technology Museum AR Books" in "Social Education" Section, click the "AR".

3 扫描部分页面中的"👁"（小眼睛图标）。

Scan the icon "👁" on some pages.

4 看图片、听语音、玩转 3D，还有精彩视频，让你全方位了解这件了不起的发明。

Find more about the amazing invention with pictures, audios and 3D videos.

姓名：爱德华·韦斯顿
身份：美国电气工程师，开发了一种可精确测量电流的
仪表，是电子测量仪器发展历史中最重要的人物之一

Name: Edward Weston

Identity: American electrical engineer, developer
of a meter to accurately measure electrical
currents, one of the most important figures in the
development of electronic measuring instruments

姓名：小科
身份：6岁的小男孩
性格：充满好奇，喜欢探索和提问，喜欢电子
科技产品

Name: Kyle

Identity: Six-year-old boy

Character: Curious, like to explore and ask
questions, fond of electronic products

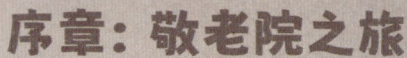

序章：敬老院之旅
INTRODUCTION: VISITING THE NURSING HOME

这天，小科和同学们来到敬老院参加学校组织的志愿者活动。当他来到病房看望一位生病的老爷爷时，床头的仪器吸引了他的注意力。老师告诉小科，这个仪器正在监测老爷爷的身体状况，上面的这些数字就是在给老爷爷的身体"打分"。

One day, Kyle and his classmates come to a nursing home as volunteers. When he visits a sick old man in the ward, the instrument beside the bed attracts his attention. The teacher tells Kyle that it's monitoring his physical condition, and the numbers on it are the "scores" of his health.

老师，为什么这台仪器上的数字就代表着老爷爷的身体状态呢？

Miss, how can the numbers on this instrument show his physical condition?

到电子科技博物馆去看看，说不定可以找到答案哦。

Go to the Electronic Science and Technology Museum. You may find the answers.

这些仪器和老爷爷床头的仪器好像啊，到底什么是电子测量呢？

These devices look like those bedside the old man's bed. What indeed is electronic measurement?

带着昨天的疑问，小科来到电子科技博物馆寻找答案。

在博物馆的电子测量仪器单元，小科发现了和昨天类似的仪器。他正在思索什么是电子测量时，一位名叫爱德华·韦斯顿的老爷爷出现了。

With the question of yesterday, Kyle comes to the Electronic Science and Technology Museum for answers.

In the Electronic Measuring Instruments section, Kyle finds a similar device. While he is wondering what electronic measurement is, an old man named Edward Weston appears.

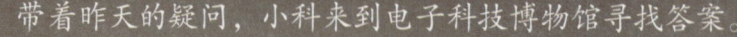

他告诉小科："我们的身体中隐藏着巨量且神秘的信息，而电子测量的一种应用就是通过特定的传感器，将这些信息转化成我们能读懂的数据。"

He tells Kyle, "There is a huge amount of mysterious information hidden in our bodies. One way to apply electronic measurement is to convert such information into data that we can understand through certain sensors."

为什么要进行电子测量?
WHY DO WE NEED ELECTRONIC MEASUREMENT?

在韦斯顿爷爷的指引下,小科进行了身体数据测量。通过这次测量,小科对自己有了新的认识。

Under the instructions of Mr. Weston, Kyle has his body data measured. After that, he knows more about himself.

测量是我们认识事物和探索事物规律的重要手段。电子测量可以将事物中蕴含的抽象信息转换为我们熟知的数字，以便人们发现事物的规律。

Measurement is an important means of understanding things and exploring the rules of things. Electronic measurement can convert the abstract information in things into numbers that we are familiar with, so that people can discover the rules of things.

这些数据能帮助我们更好地认识自己。

These data can help us know ourselves better.

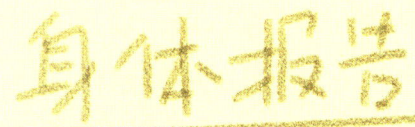

身体报告
Body Data

身高：122厘米
Height: 122 cm

心率：90次/分钟
Heart rate: 90 beats/min

体温：36摄氏度
Body temperature: 36 degrees Celsius

原来我的身体里藏着这么多数据啊！
There are so much data in my body!

身体报告
Body Data

想一想 Think

还能用电子测量仪器测出哪些身体数据呢？

What other body data can be measured with electronic measuring instruments?

电子测量发展大事记
IMPORTANT EVENTS IN THE DEVELOPMENT OF ELECTRONIC MEASUREMENT

1928

美国 Generd Radio 公司生产出世界第一批电压表。

The world's first voltmeters were produced by an American company, Generd Radio.

1952

美国 NLS（Non-Linear Systems）公司研制出电子管式四位数字电压表，开启了电子测量仪器的数字化时代。

An American company, Non-Linear Systems (NLS), developed a four-digit tube-type digital voltmeter, starting the digital era of electronic measuring instruments.

1972

英国 Nicolet 公司发明了世界上第一台数字存储示波器 DSO（digital storage oscilloscope）。

A British company, Nicolet, invented the world's first digital storage oscilloscope (DSO).

测量人体数据其实是电子测量技术发展到一定阶段后的延伸应用。电子测量技术最初主要用于测量电压、电流、电信号等。

The measurement of human body data is an extension of electronic measurement technology at a certain stage of development. The technology was first used mainly to measure voltages, currents, electrical signals, and so on.

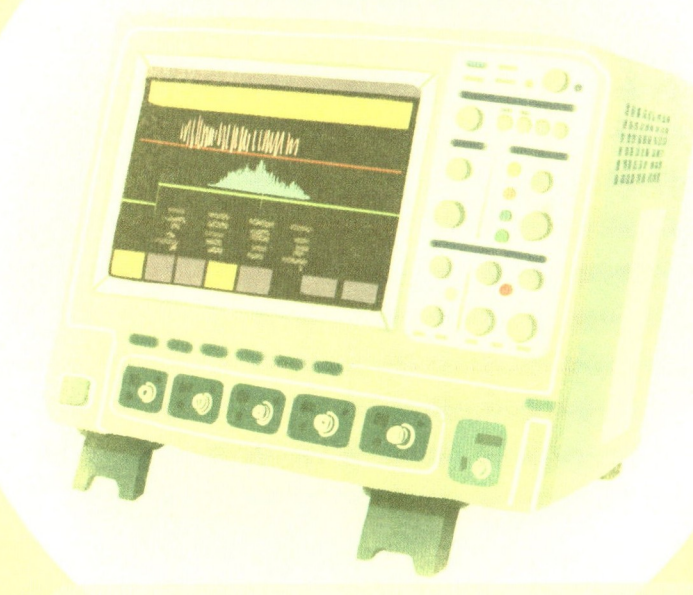

1977

美国福禄克（Fluke）公司推出世界上第一台手持式数字万用表。

An American company, Fluke, invented the world's first handheld digital multimeter.

1986

美国国家仪器公司（NI）以 LabVIEW 为软件开发平台，提出虚拟仪器技术。

An American company, National Instruments (NI), used LabVIEW as the software development platform and proposed the virtual instrument technology.

1996

美国惠普公司（HP）发明了世界上第一台混合信号示波器 MSO（mixed-signal oscilloscope）。

An American company, Hewlett-Packard (HP), invented the world's first mixed-signal oscilloscope (MSO).

电子测量历史中的里程碑——万用表
A MILESTONE IN THE HISTORY OF ELECTRONIC MEASUREMENT—MULTIMETER

20 世纪 20 年代，随着电气技术的广泛应用，人们对电子测量仪器提出了更高的要求，工程师们迫切需要一种能够测量多种电学参数的仪器。

In the 1920s, with the wide application of electrical technology, people had higher requirements for electronic measuring instruments, and engineers urgently needed an instrument to measure multiple electrical parameters.

据说第一个现代意义上的万用表是由英国邮电局的一位工程师发明的。为了维修通信设施，他在工作中需要不断测量电路中的电压、电流、电阻等。由于受不了需要同时携带多种电表的麻烦，他研制出了可以测量电压、电流和电阻的万用表，当时被称为"安伏欧万用表"。

The first modern multimeter is said to be invented by an engineer at the British Post Office. He needed to frequently measure the voltages, currents, and resistance of the circuits to maintain the communication facilities. He was tired of carrying different meters at the same time, so he developed a multimeter that could measure voltages, currents, and resistance. It was called an "Avometer" at that time.

电子测量技术的又一次进步——RLC 电桥
ANOTHER PROGRESS IN ELECTRONIC MEASUREMENT TECHNOLOGY—RLC BRIDGE

随着电子技术的发展，传统的万用表已经不能满足人们的需要，因为它只能对有限种类的器件进行测量，具有一定的局限性。这时，一种新的测量仪器诞生了，它就是 RLC 电桥。

RLC 电桥主要用于测量电阻、电容和电感，测量精度比较高，操作起来也十分简单。

With the development of electronic technology, the traditional multimeter could no longer meet people's needs, because it could only measure a limited number of devices, and had certain limitations. Then, a new measuring instrument was invented, the RLC bridge.

RLC bridges are used to measure resistance, capacitance, and inductance with high accuracy. And they are easy to operate.

RLC 电桥和万用表有什么区别呢？

What are the differences between an RLC bridge and a multimeter?

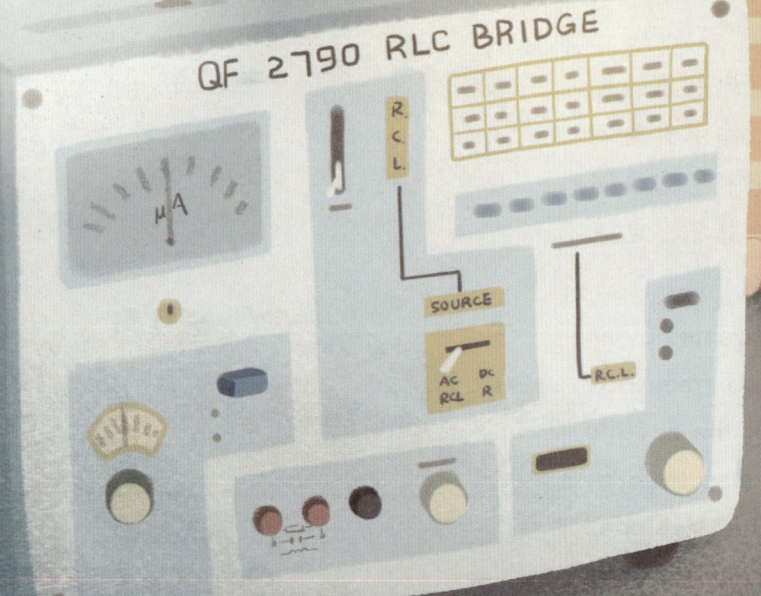

可以把RLC电桥理解为升级版的万用表。

Think of an RLC bridge as an upgraded multimeter.

电阻、电容和电感是电路中的三个基本元件，它们在电路中的作用各不相同，但都很重要。

The resistor, the capacitor, and the inductor are the three basic components of an electric circuit. They play different roles in a circuit, but are all very important.

我是电容，是一种存储电荷的元件。

I am a capacitor. I can store electric charge.

我是电感，是存储电磁能量的元件。

I am an inductor. I can store electromagnetic energy.

我是电阻，是电路中的一个基本元件，可以限制电流的流动。

I am a resistor. I'm a basic component in a circuit to restrict the flow of electricity.

看的见的信号——数字存储示波器
VISIBLE SIGNALS—DSO

数字存储示波器将电信号转化为曲线显示出来，可以让人们更清楚地看到所测信号在一段时间内信号强度的变化。

DSOs convert electrical signals into curves and display them. People can see more clearly the changes in signal strength over a period.

我们的示波器在海外也十分畅销呢。

Our oscilloscopes are also very popular overseas.

万用表和RLC电桥都是将电信号转化为准确的数据，而示波器则是把肉眼看不见的电信号变换成看得见的图像，以便人们研究各种电现象的变化过程。

在被测信号的作用下，电子束就像一支笔的笔尖，可以在屏幕上描绘出被测信号的变化曲线。

Both multimeters and RLC bridges convert electrical signals into accurate data, but oscilloscopes convert invisible electrical signals into visible images for people to study the changing processes of various electrical phenomena.

Controlled by the measured signals, the electron beam can act like the tip of a pen to draw the changing curves of the measured signals on the screen.

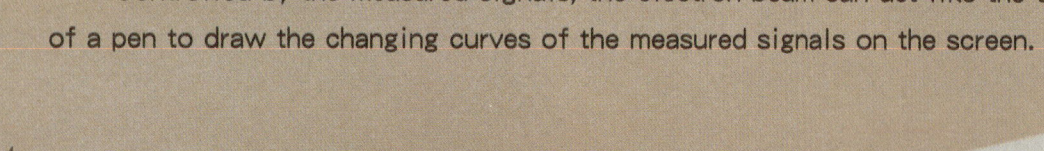

我国生产的数字示波器凭借优良的性能、高精度的测量标准和实惠的价格畅销全世界。

DSOs made in China are popular around the world for their excellent performance, high-precision standards, and affordable prices.

电子测量与遥感技术——抗震救灾用飞机

ELECTRONIC MEASUREMENT AND REMOTE SENSING—EARTHQUAKE RELIEF AIRCRAFTS

有一种应用探测仪器对远距离目标进行非接触式探测，信息提取、处理和分析的测量技术，叫作"遥感"。作为电子测量技术的新应用，人们可以通过使用飞行物上的遥感技术，接收地面物体反射或发射的电磁波信号，并以图像胶片或数据磁带的形式记录下来，以便后续对信号进行分析和处理。

There is a measuring technique called "remote sensing". It uses detection instruments for non-contact detection and information extraction, processing, and analysis of remote target. People can use this new technology on aircrafts to receive electromagnetic wave signals reflected or emitted by the objects on the ground, and record them in image films or data tapes for analysis and processing.

在"5·12"汶川大地震抗震救灾期间，电子科技大学联合有关单位组成"低空无人机高分辨率遥感灾害应急专家队"，使用无人机等设备深入地震重灾区进行勘测，获取了重点灾区受灾情况图像，并将图像传回后方指挥部，为救援团队有效开展工作提供了重要帮助。

During the "May 12" Wenchuan Earthquake relief in China, the University of Electronic Science and Technology of China (UESTC), together with other relevant organizations, formed the "Low Altitude UAV High Resolution Remote Sensing Disaster Emergency Expert Response Team". They used UAVs and other equipment to conduct surveys and collect images of the disaster-affected areas, and sent them back to the command center. This greatly helped the rescue team.

"呼，原来刚才的一切都是一场梦啊！"小科从梦中醒来，深吸了几口气。就在他伸懒腰的时候，小科注意到手腕上佩戴的智能手表上有数字在跳动，这些数字记录了他刚才的睡眠情况。小科既惊讶又欣喜，原来电子测量就在我们身边。

"Hoo, it's just a dream!" Kyle wakes up, and takes a deep breath. When he stretches his arms, he notices the digits on his smart watch flashing. They are the records of his sleep data. How amazing it is! Electronic measurement is right around us.